I Asked the Wind

A COLLECTION OF ROMANTIC POETRY

Valerie Nifora

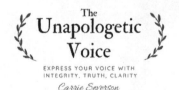

EXPRESS YOUR VOICE WITH
INTEGRITY, TRUTH, CLARITY

Carrie Severson

Published in Arizona by The Unapologetic Voice House.

I Asked the Wind
A COLLECTION OF ROMANTIC POETRY

Valerie Nifora

Published by The Unapologetic Voice House
5101 N Casa Blanca Scottsdale AZ 85253

ISBN: 9781733419727

e-ISBN: 9781733419734

Library of Congress Control Number: 2019911620

TO ALAN —

MY NORTH STAR,

MY ALWAYS…

LOVE

LOVE IS THE MEETING PLACE
OF TWO ETERNITIES

—Francisco

CONTENTS

FOREWORD

If William Shakespeare and Elizabeth Barrett Browning somehow met at a time traveler's café, fell into an impassioned romance, and later had a love child, she might write a bit like Valerie Nifora. In today's age of fast-food thinking, attention-deficit scanning, and thumb scrolls past clickbait, it's refreshing to find a relatable, digestible read that harkens back to an era of leather-bound literature's reign in terms of meter and word choice. Val has always had an open eye and an open heart for the world around her, so it's high time for those observations to dance on pages through her lens and let the reader ride shotgun against the backdrop of love's twists, turns, mysteries, and virtues. Though I've known of Val's writing skills for decades, I approached the wobbly topic of love with the tacit reticence of a card-carrying misanthrope. It never felt better to be wrong. And I'm heartened we get to read snippets of her memories and experiences that so many of us fail or fear to put into words.

Amaani F. Lyle

Military journalist, social media manager

PREFACE

A long time ago, in the very same galaxy, ten-year-old me sat down at my mom's dining room table, pencil in hand, and wrote my very first short scene ("sketch" or "skit" are synonymous terms). My friends loved my poems and parodies, so they were more than happy to perform my little skit.

I met Val at Emerson College in Boston where she auditioned for a sketch show I produced and directed. We shared the same love for comedy, *Star Trek: The Next Generation* and our homes on Long Island. Val's strong comedy instinct was apparent. Casting her started our long and colorful friendship.

Val is the type to never give up on a plan or dream. It's no surprise to me that Val has become a published author. She was always reading, writing, acting, or doing something otherwise creative when she wasn't working her tail off. She is also the hardest working person I know.

What did surprise me was Val's vulnerability. She is a strong, funny Long Island girl, but after she took me to see *Four Weddings and a Funeral* twice, I understood there was another side to Val — one that yearned for the deepness and connection that comes with sex and love, and possibly that who yearned for it from Hugh Grant.

It's with great pride that I read her poetry and lived through her love, lust, and feelings of sinful release.

When a funny person writes a funny book (which she will someday), it's expected, it's light, you laugh a little. Val's poetry goes deeper than that — into a mosaic of sensuality that leaves you hearing love as if it were a song.

These poems will inspire you to write or live deeper, in the places that may embarrass your parents. It's a journey to your whole being.

Myra Jo Martino
Writers Guild Award winner for *Ugly Betty*

INTRODUCTION

Fifteen years ago, my friend handed me a journal. The cover was a John William Waterhouse painting, "The Beautiful Lady Without Pity," with the word "Love." It sat on my desk for a while. What is "love" really? The empty pages mocked me — waiting.

And one day, as I sat there crying over my heart breaking, the strangest thing happened: these tiny little words and rhythm came out of the ether. They knocked gently on my mind at first, but upon being sufficiently ignored, they succeeded in having me grab a pencil and scribble them down. There it was — the first poem about love — failed love as it happened. It claimed its space on the page, breathing as if it was meant to be there. But I hid the journal. I buried it deep in the bottom of my closet so no one would ever find it. There, I thought. It is done with. But it's funny how things sometimes go unfinished.

What you hold in your hand now is a collection of my memories. Fifteen years of love and loss. I remember when I wrote each poem; who I wrote it about; what I felt when I wrote it.

Be gentle when you read them. They belong to you now. I hope that you find a kinship in reading them. And I wish you much love in all things, and the happiest ever after there ever was…

ABOUT THE COVER

My cousin Elias Grammatikogiannis took this picture. It is right outside our mothers' house in the village of Kallithea, which is roughly thirty-one miles from Agrinio in Greece. If you were to stand in that spot, right behind you would be the house that our grandfather built out of stone on the slope of the mountain. Straight ahead on the road carved out of the mountain is our mothers' cousin's house.

The children are a brother and a sister. What I love so much about the photograph is the little girl is resolute in her mission, while the little boy is distracted. I have no idea what made the little boy turn his head and look like he wanted to move in another direction. But, no! His sister holding his hand firmly is staying on the path. They have a journey to take together in this life, and they will take it.

For me, that is the best description of love. It is the uncompromising promise, of keeping each other on the proper path. As Saint Thomas Aquinas once said, "Love is willing the good of the other."

PART I

I LOVE YOU. ETERNAL.

I love you. Eternal.

Until time does cease.

For in your soul,

I have found,

Perfect peace.

SWING ME ROUND

Swing me round

In this dance

Leave me breathless

In a trance

Let the laughter

Spin us still

Round and round

Against our will.

Let the light

Flash on by

To fill the darkness

In the sky

Let us fall

Still in embrace

To vanish slowly

Without a trace.

THIS PERFECT THING

This perfect thing

Which God has made

To bind man and wife

Which shall not fade.

To bind two hearts

And make them whole

To add such Grace

To fill two souls.

When all this work

Has been done

To make the two

Live as one.

IF EVER PURE LOVE

If ever pure love,

There was to be,

It is that I have,

Found it in thee.

IF THIS IS NOTHING
BUT A DREAM

If this is nothing

But a dream

Then please

Wake me not.

My heart has suffered

Far too long

I do not know

Its lot.

So, please let me

Rest awhile

And breathe

With you beside.

Let the daydreams

Come and go

For in shadows

They hide.

LET ME LIE HERE A LITTLE LONGER

Let me lie here a little longer

And dream of what cannot be.

Let me rest my head upon your chest

And feel you breathe with me.

Let me hear your heart beat faster

And then, slow down its pace

Let me feel your gentle hands

And melt in your embrace.

Do not stir and wake me, dear

And shatter my illusion

Let us stay ever still

And live in this delusion.

QUIET DOWN

Quiet down,

Don't beat so fast.

Let us make,

This moment last.

Pounding, pounding,

Ever steeper,

Falling, falling,

Sinking deeper.

Shattered hearts,

Binding, turning.

Soul and body,

Ever yearning.

Silence! Stop!

And heart be still.

To gather strength

And keep our will.

WHEN YOU PLACE
YOUR HAND UPON MY CHEST

When you place your hand

Upon my chest,

To feel the beating of my heart.

My soul leaps forth

To reach for yours

To vow we'll never part.

When you place your lips

Upon my brow

To feel the warmth of my face,

My body yearns

To melt with yours

To vanish from this place.

When I place my hand,

Upon your cheek

And feel the softness of your skin,

Our hearts begin

To beat as one

To live in passion's sin.

THE LACES

Love, rub your fingers

Across my cheek

And just undo the laces.

Let it drop to the ground

And take me to the places

Where only you

Touch my soul

Let the world stop still

Release me not from your grasp

Simply take my will.

TWIRL ME ROUND

Hold my hand and twirl me round

Let not my feet touch the ground

Let not my heart stop its pace

Let no laughter leave my face

In this moment of no fears

To live out my earthly years.

KISS ME GENTLY

Kiss me gently

And ask me not to speak

Through that tenderness

You'll find the answers

That you seek.

Mock me not bitterly

For words I will not say

And let each moment pass

Into a dawning day.

Act not angrily

And judge me not too stern

For in my heart you will find

All for which you deeply yearn.

Tell me tenderly

That your love will always be

So, I can untie the binds

And let my soul be free.

UPON YOUR LEAVING

Upon your leaving

The earth does cease

And fragrant flowers

Bloom their last release.

Upon your leaving

My heart grows cold

And mirth and gladness

From my lips last told.

Upon your leaving

My soul grows dark

No song can fill it

No chime, no lark.

Upon your leaving

There is no light.

I dwell in darkness

In moonless night.

TOUCH ME GENTLY

Touch my cheek gently

But do not wipe the tear

In that tiny salted thing

Evaporates my fear.

When you are with me

Standing by my side

All the shadows lift

Nowhere for them to hide.

Illuminate my heart

And let it all burn bright

With you as my sun

I will never live in night.

LET'S RUN OUR FINGERS THROUGH THE SAND

Come, my love
And hold my hand
Let's run our fingers
Through the sand.

And watch the tides
Roll from the sea
And feel your heartbeat
Close to me.

Let clouds drift by
And seagulls soar
Dreams of distant days
And lore.

To feel the sun
Upon my face
Huddled close
In warm embrace.

The gods may send
Down wind or storm
And sands may rise
Against our form,

But let us stay
Until time does cease
In close embrace
In perfect peace.

LET THE CLOCK HAND
KEEP ITS TIME

Let the clock hand
Keep its time
Let its bell ring
Let it chime.

Let the moon face
Pass above
Let it watch us
Close, my love.

Let the darkness
Come and pass
Let it creep
Through window glass.

Let the seasons
Change and turn
Let them make
This hard earth yearn.

Let them all do
As they need
Mind them not
Pay no heed.

Let us stand here
Heart made whole
Bound together
As one soul.

COME HOLD MY HAND, LOVE

Come, hold my hand, Love

Even if it is for an hour

Even if from above

The fates do not smile fondly.

Come sit with me, Dear

Even in the dark shadows

Even with our parting near

Stay with me a bit longer.

And when you leave me

To venture forth beyond

Deep through forest and sea

Do not think upon us.

For silently I will stay

Frozen here in this moment

Until the end of day

Forever empty for the loss.

PART II

THE SADNESS

When I stare sadly into your eyes

And see treasures untold

I know that this is a world

I shall never behold.

In that majesty and glory

Where your heart does live

In that gentle kindness

That knows but to give.

I cannot tread there

My soul, it is too weak

For such is the damnation

And perils of the meek.

LOVE HIDE NOT
YOUR FACE FROM ME

Love, hide not

Your face from me

And hide not

In the dark.

For even in

A midnight hour

One might hear

A lark.

Forgive yourself

My Love

As I have

So done.

And let not

This little thing

Hide you

From the sun.

I DO NOT KNOW

I placed my head

On your shoulder

And it felt cold.

Your grasp was weak

So I asked,

"Will we grow old?"

"I don't know,"

You whispered

Staring at the sky.

A lightning bug

Flew past us.

"Maybe we'll just die."

I SIT HERE SILENTLY

And so I sit here

Silently

And listen to the clock.

And wonder how

I have become

A thing that one would mock.

You've left me barren

Frozen over

Like ice upon a lake.

How am I to survive?

Forever gone

My heart you did take.

IT IS NOT FAIR

My love

It is not fair

To leave me here

Alone

Without a heart.

To fill

My somber days

With endless tears

Empty

And far apart.

Please come

Lift my soul

Release my fears

Free

Like from the start.

IT WILL NOT BE

And so, my love, it will not be.

The earth does take your life from me.

No longer to stare upon your face.

And feel your breath in quickened pace.

WIND THAT BLOWS

Wind that blows through the trees

Take away that which grieves

Cast it out to the sea

Far, far away from me.

DO YOU KNOW HOW SLOWLY

Love, you do not know how slowly

The time does pass?

Each day the clock hand winds itself

And I am left a mass

That is weak and hollow,

A heart that is like glass.

Darling, when will you release me?

Come and bring me life.

Eliminate the emptiness.

Eliminate this strife

That leaves a body and soul

Severed like a knife.

LEAVE ME IN MY SORROW

Leave me in my sorrow

Leave me in my despair

Do not reach with your gentle touch

And lift me to the air.

Leave me in my anger

Leave me in my night

Do not grasp me with your hand

And bring me to the light.

Leave me in my shadow

Leave me with my tears

Breathe not your breath upon my face

And vanquish all my fears.

HOSTILITY

Darling, there's no need for hostility
The kind you always aim at me
The kind that keeps you silently
Wallowing in your temper.

For once, can't you let it be?
Let anger just pass from me
Let it all end tranquilly
And let me feel loved.

No. You aim your tongue willingly
Sharper than a knife can be
Sharper, still forcefully,
You pierce my heart.

ANGER, FILL THE AIR

Anger, anger, fill the air

And do not miss a drop

Fill my lungs as I breathe

And fill them to the top.

Do not utter but a word

And loose intoxication

Let it linger with your blood

Love's inoculation.

DO NOT MOCK ME

Do not mock me

With your grin

And whimsy

As you dance.

Darkness can

Creep from the clouds

Where sun lived

By chance.

Do not pretend

To care for me

And pick flowers

By your hill.

You took that

Which mattered

And left me

Without will.

NOT A WORD

You do not want to hear from me

Not one little word.

You want to live as you have

In a world quite absurd.

Where only pain can touch you

And your wounds never heal.

Ah, it is condemned I am

With chains without appeal.

YOUR SILENCE

Your silence
Devastates completely
All I long to be.

It casts nothing
But hollowness
Deep inside of me.

POUNDING WAVE

Pounding wave and sifting sand,

Boldly, I reach to grab your hand.

And though a dark cloud does turn,

Steady heartbeat as I yearn,

Alone in wind, I will be,

An ocean's distance for you and me.

PART III

I CRIED FOR YOU

I cried for you

Again today

Until my eyes

Turned red.

A melancholy

So thick

I could not lift

My head.

And yet,

If here you were

In full form

Complete.

I would tremble

Empty still

And fall before

Your feet.

I DID LOVE YOU

But, love, I did love you
And let my soul go bare
And peeled away my flesh for you
Beyond what I could spare.

And, love, I still love you
But cannot take the pain
I have bled myself dry
And nothing can remain.

So, please do not be angry
And forgive me, if you might
I am left with nothing now
A cold and darkened night.

BROKEN GLASS

I wish I could discard you
Just like a broken glass
Like you have done of me
And left behind what's passed.

I wish I could just leave you
And purge my heart and flee
The memories they do nothing
But simply circle me.

Go! Be!
And fly into the wind
Do not look back and think
That only I have sinned.

LOOK NOT AT ME WICKEDLY

Look not at me wickedly

And smile like a thief.

It is a thing that will not be

A thing of false belief.

If faith can cure me, Darling

Then so let it be.

For in this midnight hour

Let peace be here with me.

CIRCLES

Circles seem so ever winding.

Souls keep forever binding.

Whisper gently! Do not speak!

Jagged hearts will wound the meek.

Grab your sword and into battle.

Do not shun the bones that rattle.

Anon! Anon! Another day is dawning.

Underneath, the dark earth yawning.

DON'T WORRY ABOUT MY TEARS

Don't worry about my tears

They are nothing, Love.

They are nothing like

The cold blade of the spear

You thrust into my heart.

Don't worry about the scar.

It is nothing, Dear.

It is nothing like

The pit so deep

That grows between us.

Don't worry about me.

I am nothing, Dear.

I am nothing like

What you can see

Out there in your world.

A LITTLE WORD

A little word flew into the room,

And it did flutter by,

First a whisper it did say,

Quietly — "Why?"

It started to bang about,

And louder it did cry.

In shock, I stood and stared.

Shouting loudly — "WHY?"

The shrieks too much to bear,

Fists clenched, eyes shut, stood I.

Tears flowing down my face

Persisting — "WHY? WHY? WHY?"

SO LITTLE

Why, my love
Should I give you
My heart
When you have done
So little

But treat it
Like a block
Of wood
For you to simply
Whittle?

You sharpen still
Your carver's knife
Prepared
To start again
Anew.

Even still
You search it deep
To find a cut
That's true.

TO BICKER

Darling, this is silliness that does make us bicker.

Idle tongues that take their pace ever quicker.

For it is such somberness we bring,

Like muted nightingales that will not sing.

So let the evening in silence pass.

And awaken tomorrow, hand with glass.

THE CHOICE

Ah, what a fickle thing this is.

This love which burrows so deep,

And interferes with a mind,

Dashing dreams one is to keep.

Alas, it strikes its icy grasp,

And wonders not how strong,

But, fearlessly it holds its clasp,

Withering life gone wrong.

Fie! What is one to ask?

How loud is one to cry?

For solemnly one's left to mourn,

When a heart poisoned goes awry.

SILENT DRUM

Your silence
Beats a drum
That echoes.

It vibrates
With no sound.
It penetrates
Inside my heart
It knows no bounds.

Your silence
Clouds the sun
That shines.

It darkness
All the flowers.
It leaves no
Petal untouched.
It blocks the
Warming showers.

Your silence
Devastates completely
All I long to be

It casts nothing
But hollowness
Deep inside of me.

BURN MY HEART

Fire! Fire! Burn my heart

And dash it to the sea.

Take away all that is,

And drown my memories.

Break apart this weary flesh,

And smash it into the stone.

When this is all complete

Leave me nothing but a bone.

I ASKED THE WIND

I asked the wind
His name again,
And, he would not reply.

He danced around
And touched my cheek
And let out a gentle sigh.

"O, Wind!
Do not be coy!
And laugh at my dismay!
Appear! Speak!
And grab my hand
Let us both away!"

At this the wind
Stopped his frolic.
A branch did not move.

The stillness! Quiet!
I held my breath.
He did not approve.

A FOOL

A fool and I are quite the same
In love we both believe.
And just in a simple jest
You do blithely deceive.

Kiss not the gentle wind
And blow them not at me,
For even he who was blind,
In Grace can learn to see.

Gather all your trinkets, Love,
And leave them upon your path
Wander ever swiftly, Dear,
And feel not my seething wrath.

UNSAID

So many words they go unsaid,

They simply echo in my head.

Repeat, repeat, but not aloud.

In vast caverns they will abound.

Crashing up against my tongue.

Until you leave; they go unsung.

THE RING

How dare you come

And take away

That which does

Make me sing?

A foolish thing

Encircled gold.

Engraved and

But a ring.

You will not

Shackle me

With this band

You give.

I will not be

Bound by force.

My soul will beat

And live.

GRAVE MISFORTUNE

What grave misfortune

This thing called time

That breaks a heart

In two.

It dallies idly

On the clouds

To vex that which

Is true.

Damn the pendulum

As it ticks

To dawn the day

Anew.

And damn still

This foolish heart

That ever did

Love you.

DANCE UPON THE AISLE

Wear your white dress

And dance upon the aisle

Do not turn to look for me

Not for a little while.

Dream today,

And dance without heed.

For I know in your heart

Lurks a dark seed.

WHY DO YOU TORTUE SO?

Ah, Love, why do you torture so,

With a word that binds and mangles?

With minds and hearts ever fleeting,

Entwined and left in tangles?

Can you not be true?

Can you not confess your heart?

But leave me tortured and beaten bare,

Each time we are to part?

What is this glory that you hold?

What is this thing you are seeking?

To leave a man a hollow shell

And take his soul for your keeping.

HOW DOES IT FEEL?

How does it feel

To be standing with her

And not with me?

Was it because

I wanted you

Before you wanted me?

YOU ASK ME IF I LOVED YOU

You ask me if I loved you
To that I will not reply
For whichever way I answer
It simply is a lie.

Seasons change in earnest
And flowers bloom anew
And so too emotions
Fickle and never true.

Everything has passed now
Like shadows on a cloud
And never do I want to hear
Your name spoken aloud.

PEN TO PAPER

I put my pen to paper

To write while I was away.

But my words did leave me

I had not much to say.

I rambled phrases in my head

And stared at sun and moon.

Time simply passed along

And arrived far too soon.

I find now that I see you

I squandered every day

And if my strength were gathered

I would be on my way.

IF I WERE TO WHISPER
TO THE WIND

If I were to whisper to the wind

The things I long to say

Would it bring them back to you

And leave me in dismay?

Would you take my confessions

And dash them to despair

And laugh ever heartfully

Echoing in the air?

I DIE

And so you fade gently

Into my memory.

But the power

Of your presence will not leave me

With you I felt ever alive.

And as you drift away, I die.

DID YOU LOVE ME?

Is it true,

That you ever were — my beloved

Or perhaps —

It was the light of your cigarette

That fell from your fingers?

Yes. Perhaps it was but ashes.

EPILOGUE

YOUR FACE

Your face

Came to my mind today

And so

Made me smile.

I listened

To your gentle voice

And wandered

For a while.

Eyes closed

I dreamed quietly

Of what

We once were.

Gone now

Time has passed

My heart's

Saboteur.

#Storiesthrupoetry

I believe in the power of stories. I believe in their power to bind the human existence together. I believe in their power to inspire, to transform, to uplift, and to enlighten. And in this book are my stories. Fifteen years of experience with love.

I hope in reading these little stories I've shared — these little glimpses into my heart — that you find you are not alone. None of us is alone really. We belong to this wonderful tapestry called life. And life is about love, isn't it?

You can find me on Instagram @valerienifora and share your stories through poetry with #storiesthrupoetry. I look forward to seeing you there.

ABOUT THE AUTHOR

To learn more about me please visit my website
at www.valerienifora.com

You'll find blogs and social inspirational posts and lots more.
Come visit! And let me know what you think.

You can also find me at:

@valerienifora

Valerie Nifora

vnifora

https://www.linkedin.com/in/vnifora/

PHOTO CREDITS